The Power of
Organizational Resilience:

How to Retain Talent
and Increase Your Bottom Line

Rasheda Hatchett, MN, RN

Table of Contents

Introduction

When the individuals that make up a team possess the quality of resilience, they are not only better at their respective jobs; they collectively make the team stronger. As a leader, it can be challenging to create a resilient culture within your organization, but it is one of the single most important priorities you can choose to focus on. However, many leaders are not even thinking about resilience as an implementable solution. One of the biggest misconceptions I hear about resilience is, *"you either have it, or you don't."* To me this sounds oddly like a copout, an admission that once a staff is established, there is nothing to do but accept your lot and work with what you have, even if that means working with one hand tied behind your back. However, nothing could be further from the truth. Resilience is a trait that

Resilience is a trait that can be learned, practiced and mastered.

can be learned, practiced and mastered. It can be mastered on the individual level, and it can be woven into the fabric of your organization so that employees consistently function at their best. Once this is accomplished, resilience can become the backbone of your organization's culture, regardless of whether it is present there today or not. On some level, I'm sure that there are ways in which your organization already promotes resilience, whether purposely or not. This book will help you identify the areas of growth within your organization; it will show you how to capitalize on these golden opportunities to shift your organizational culture and increase employee engagement and satisfaction, all while decreasing turnover and saving costs.

But why exactly is resilience so important? What is it about this one, fairly elusive, quality that leads to such dramatic outcomes when it comes to workplace performance? To answer that, let's think about what resilience really means with an example. If you're like most of the world, you likely always have your Smartphone close at hand; but this wasn't always the case. If you go back fifteen years, we were just getting used to these personal phones. And in doing so, we were constantly dropping and losing them. It seems in the early days, we were always dealing with cracked screens, devices dropped in water and misplaced phones. These problems are far less commonplace today, but it's not because we are less distracted or more careful with our phones; it's because the phones themselves have become more resilient. We have cases that protect our screens, the phones are equipped with tech that allows them to be submerged in water for various periods of time and even when we lose them, we can find our phones with other apps and devices. Carrying a phone worth hundreds of dollars was once an incredibly risky proposition, but now it's riskier to leave home without it. And the reason is because we've made this costly device more resilient.

Resilient individuals are just as valuable (if not more valuable) than resilient smartphones. They have the ability to bounce back from adversity quickly and without a significant change in attitude. They accept setbacks as a part of life, and so aren't unreasonably affected when setbacks inevitably arise. Because they recognize that disappointment does happen, they don't attach their wellbeing to their expectations and therefore recover from disappointment promptly. They also adapt to changes of any kind better than their non-resilient counterparts. All of these skills leave them with the capacity to cope and even thrive in stressful situations. And of course, work is one of the most stressful environments that we as humans, encounter in our daily lives. Work is unpredictable, brimming with potential setbacks and ripe for change all the time. So in short, if you are not resilient, you are suddenly a pretty big liability.

These qualities translate into the workplace in a variety of ways. Voluntary employee turnover is a $1 trillion-dollar problem in the U.S.[1] While some employees are simply looking for a new role, others leave due to the culture of unappreciation within the organization, specifically 79% cited this as the main reason for their separation.[2] This kind of lack of appreciation can result in burnout and cause an employee to be less motivated or to leave the organization altogether. Employees who are less resilient are more prone to burnout, and burnt out employees cost organizations money in ways that we'll get into later on.

For these reasons, creating organizational resilience should be top of mind for every leader, especially as we navigate this new normal and begin to explore the new ways in which we can add value to our teams. Additionally, the individuals on your team need to be personally resilient in order to face everyday obstacles effectively and to excel at their job. As a leader, it is up to you to create a resilient-friendly culture by consistently modeling resilient behaviors and helping your team understand the important role resilience plays in building a

As a leader, it is up to you to create a resilient-friendly culture by consistently modeling resilient behaviors

lasting, trusted brand. After all, organizational resilience is the secret sauce to employee retention, reduced burnout, positive stakeholder relations, increased client satisfaction, higher employee satisfaction rates, and ongoing employee turnover cost savings.

Creating a resilient culture within your organization helps build employee confidence in the system. When the surrounding culture is supportive, employees implicitly understand that the organization will survive and thrive despite the challenges it faces. Imagine how confidently your team will go into meetings with potential partners when they know as an organization, you are committed to thriving and willing to innovate to meet the needs of your customers. Having confidence in the organization that is behind you is an invaluable tool when it comes to completing tasks successfully. But this confidence isn't a given; it has to be earned.

Now I want you to imagine an environment where your team is going above and beyond for your clients with client satisfaction ratings consistently in the upper 90%, product and service reviews trending at 4.5 star ratings, employee satisfaction rates are high and turnover is low. As a leader of the organization, you know that this translates to hundreds of thousands and even millions of dollars in tangible revenue and cost savings. This is certainly the dream, but it does not actually have to be a dream. Suppose I told you that effective leadership and creating a culture of resilience had the power to make this dream an effective business strategy that garners real results. Knowing that, would you implement the strategy? I'm sure that as an astute leader, you'd be willing to do whatever it takes to assure your brand was producing high quality results, staying relevant, and providing excellent service both internally and externally.

This guide is going to show you the steps you can take to create organizational resilience in your workplace and will lay out the cost saving measures you need to implement in order to take your organization from ordinary to thriving. As the landscape of how we do business, how we lead, how we hire, how we retain talented team members, and even how we simply live our day-to-day lives changes, it's time to dig into cultivating a culture of resilience as a remedy for our rapidly changing organizational needs.

Burnout

In nursing, the undying flame of Florence Nightingale's lamp represents the selfless urge to care, help, advocate, and sacrifice for the people we serve. As time has gone on, I've watched as parts of this philosophy have bled into so many other arenas of the work. In some ways, it's as if we've taken this message too far, sacrificing our own health and wellbeing for the sake of the job. But because so many of us are burning this literal midnight oil for the wellbeing of our patents and leaving no room for self-care, we are left feeling purposeless, exhausted and unappreciated. We are burning out instead of blazing full steam ahead in the direction of Nightingale.

The American Psychological Association defines burnout as, "physical, emotional, or mental exhaustion accompanied by decreased motivation, lowered performance, and negative attitudes toward oneself and others."[3] Throughout our careers, we've all seen burnout symptoms in a co-worker, employee or even ourselves, yet despite our intimate knowledge of burnout, it is unlikely that we've ever been offered a burnout assessment tool or been asked by a leader if we are experiencing burnout. Why? If it is so common, then why haven't we heard more about its prevalence and been exposed to more prevention measures? Why have some leaders never seen a burnout assessment? When I ask this question of organization leaders in my workshops, the most common response is, *"I didn't know I could offer that."* When I ask these leaders what they have offered their employees in terms of burnout, the room goes silent. And that is exactly my point.

Now, this alarming lack of an answer is not because people don't care if their employees are experiencing burnout. I can tell from the reactions of the people at my workshops that this oversight is devastating to them. The main reason for this oversight is that the leaders within the organization never saw it as their responsibility to help prevent and manage burnout. Yes, they saw that it impacted the schedule, the organization's effectiveness, and the bottom line, but it was accepted as something that couldn't be changed, as a cost of doing business. They believed that there was no real way to control how the individuals on your team would react to adversity, and so you just had to sort of hope for the best.

As it turns out, leaders do have the power to improve the resilience of their team members, thereby reducing the prevalence of burnout in their organization. The number one way to prevent and manage burnout is simply to assess it. After all, you can't fix what you don't know is broken. Assessing your employees is the first step to understanding where they are, what motivates them, what stresses them out, and what they need to succeed. Using an assessment tool that gauges where they stand on assertions like, "I feel misunderstood or unappreciated by my coworkers," or "I have negative thoughts about my job," can help you get an

As it turns out, leaders do have the power to improve the resilience of their team members, thereby reducing the prevalence of burnout in their organization.

9

accurate sense of where your workers are at emotionally, and it can give direction when it comes to addressing the problem. Armed with this information, you can start to put strategies and procedures in place that help your staff and improve the success of your organization. These sorts of tools can be used in two different ways. You can dispatch them anonymously as a way to plan professional development and see where your employees need the most help, or you can use it as a quarterly check-in tool to ensure you're catching burnout early enough so that you can begin working on interventions before problems progress too far. In this new normal, it's critical to begin looking for innovative ways to add value for your employees. The creation of professional development strategies that are focused on helping teams cope with the changing demands of todays business world are the perfect way to stand out in a crowded and changing marketplace.

Why is it important to assess burnout?

You might be wondering why assessing burnout is so important. Could it really be at the root of so many workplace metrics? A recent study found that nearly 77% of all work professionals suffer from burnout, and 84% of millennials surveyed say they're suffering from burnout. [4] As a leader, if your numbers are anywhere close to these, you probably also recognize that you're not functioning well as an organization. Burnout affects both internal and external relationships. An employee who is either on the cusp of burnout or who is experiencing clear burnout is not as productive as their resilient counterparts, and is likely exhibiting some of the physical, behavioral, or emotional symptoms of burnout on a daily basis. We will breakdown what these symptoms are in the next chapters. But what is true, is that it is our role as leaders to help ease burnout symptoms, and the way to do it is by providing education and strategies that our employees can implement to improve their work and personal lives. When our employees function better, the entire organization runs more efficiently and effectively. It's a win-win.

An employee who is either on the cusp of burnout or who is experiencing clear burnout is not as productive as their resilient counterparts

Workplace burnout comes in many different forms, and can be attributed to a variety of causes. Sometimes it stems from the kinds of clients we are serving. When our clients are struggling to provide for their families and to take care of their own basic needs like housing and safety, we can internalize those anxieties. When we are charged with caring for patients who have complex medical needs, we sometimes end up taking that load on personally. Other forms of burnout happen because the stress of our corporate position is brimming with intense deadlines, demanding clients, and high leadership expectations and there is no corresponding sense of support from the organization. This is why the need for burnout prevention and management extends across the continuum of working roles. There is no one area that is protected from the damages of burnout. With the addition of the pandemic to our plates, we are in a very unique time and circumstance. There is so much coming at us from so many directions. We're trying to juggle being an employee and leader, with being a parent, caregiver to aging parents, and so much more. This expansion of roles, along with our own self-inflicted expectations contributes to burnout. It's a major reason why your team members are often overwhelmed even before they log on to see what's waiting for them in their inbox. As leadership, we must take the nature of the current environment into account when checking in with our team. The people who work for us are not one-dimensional taskmasters; they are complex, talented individuals who are doing their best to manage a plethora of tasks at once, and they need our support in this role.

The True Cost of Burnout

As a leader, it's important to note that burnout is more than just a term tossed around as a synonym for "stressed." The World Health Organization has even added it to its International Classification of Diseases. They go on to pinpoint three characteristics of burnout to include, energy depletion or exhaustion, increased negativity or cynicism toward the job, and a decreased professional efficacy. [5] When these factors are taken into

when employees are succumbing to burnout in droves, it becomes a big financial burden pretty quickly.

account, it's clear to any employer that there is an actual monetary cost to burnout. So when employees are succumbing to burnout in droves, it becomes a big financial burden pretty quickly.

Let's consider these points:

- When it comes to the healthcare-related costs of burnout, it adds up to between $125 billion and $190 billion annually in the U.S.[6]

- According to Gallup, a disengaged employee has a 37% higher absenteeism rate, an 18% lower productivity rate, and is 15% less profitable than an engaged coworker. This means a loss of 34% of per salary. That means, for every $10,000 you pay a disengaged worker, consider $3,400 lost.[7]

- Conservatively, burnout is responsible for 20-50% of employee turnover. According to the Work Institute's 2020 Retention Report, the cost of employee turnover is $15,000 per employee. This number is based on the median income for a salary worker ($48,672 in 2020); and it's estimated that the cost of turnover comes to 30% of the full salary.

Earlier we mentioned that 77% of the workforce is experiencing burnout. If this is the case across the board, in all industries and places of work, then it would be safe to say this percentage carries over into your workplace as well. So let's do a simple math equation just to illustrate the point.

Let's say there are 100 employees in your organization. By these numbers, 77 of those employees are experiencing burnout. They aren't as productive as you'd like, they tend to not show up when you need them, they are often partaking in client interactions that are subpar, and they are overall far less efficient than your ideal employee. But what you may not have calculated is just how much they are costing you.

Let's say that you manage to retain all 77 of those burnt out workers. They all receive a salary of $50k annually, but they are operating at reduced capacity so according to the numbers above, that is costing you 34% of their respective salaries. One employee making 50K costs you $17,000 dollars annually. Multiply that by 77, and you get just over $1.3 million dollars ($1,309,000).

Now say you experience the turnover that is expected based on the Work Institutes 2020 Retention report, showing over 27% of the workforce left their jobs in 2019 a number that's been trending upward[8]. For this illustration we'll use just some of the categories that were present.

This would mean that of your 100 employees, you can expect to lose:

- 13 from burnout (20- 50% employee loss annually)

- 5 due to insufficient career development (20% employee loss annually)

- 3 due to poor leadership (12% employee loss annually)

- 3 due to poor work/life balance (12% employee loss annually)

- 2 due to the job characteristics (10% employee loss annually)

- 1 due to poor work environment (6% employee loss annually)

Now as it turns out, all of these reasons that are not identified as burnout specifically, actually contribute to burnout; however, based on the definition of burnout, these all fit the criteria. With that being said, let's imagine that we lose 13 of the 77 burnt out employees that we expect are working in our organization. The rest of the losses come from the 23 supposed productive workers who are picking up the slack as you recruit, hire, and train the replacement employees. It won't be long before those workers begin to feel the burn as well. This means that you still have 73 employees working at diminished capacity. A cost of $1,241,000. You also have a loss of 27 workers which includes those who left due to burnout and those who left to due to burnout related reasons.

The cost to replace and train the new hires to expected standards costs $15,000 per employee. Multiply that by 27 and you get $405,000. Add that to the $1.24 million you are already spending on the burnt-out workers and you get over $1.6 million. And these numbers are an estimate, most often, your real-life scenario would have to allow for more variation in salary and could very easily be higher.

Not to mention, that if you don't have any policies and procedures in place to combat employee burnout, the same situation is going to continue happening year after year. Once you get a new group of employees trained and functioning, it will only be a matter of time before they themselves burn out, and the cycle starts all over again.

Therefore, it seems that the only surefire way to address burnout and stop this hemorrhaging of cash is to rethink the organizational systems you have in place in order to prevent burnout from happening in the first place. Luckily burnout is a very preventable problem, but it doesn't just happen magically. It takes diligence, work and a commitment to constant improvement. Sometimes you may not get it right, but if you are constantly looking to your employees for feedback, you will learn what's working and what isn't in real time, and you can adjust as you needs arise. The overall premise is quite simple: create an environment where your employees feel supported and valued, where they can be open about any stress they are feeling because they know it will be heard, understood and addressed. In the next chapters, we will go through exactly how to do this.

Luckily burnout is a very preventable problem, but it doesn't just happen magically.

Identifying Burnout

All of this sounds good if we were starting a new organization. Of course, in that case, we would set out to hire only the best people, and we'd ensure that we'd treat those people fairly. But most of us work in organizations that are already formed, with staff that is already set in their ways, and with a fully formed notion of how the organization sees them. How do we change an organization mid-stride?

The only way to do this is to first assess your current situation; and that starts with individually connecting with every single employee. You need to determine where everyone stands, and you can use the various burnout assessments tools at your disposal to do so. You can't begin to address a problem without first understanding what you're looking at. But even before you implement anything, you can start by simply observing. What do you see when you look at the individuals in your organization? Are they energized by their jobs, speaking in positive language about their day-to-day experiences, and connecting well with their coworkers? You can learn a lot about your staff if you know what to look for.

Burnout generally presents in one of three ways: emotional, behavioral, and physical. When you are able to recognize these signs in your team, you will be able to address them and take the next steps to help your employees come back from burnout. Let's take a look at emotional signs of burnout first.

Emotional Signs of Burnout

One of the most noticeable and prevalent emotional signs of burnout is when you notice an employee has adopted a cynical outlook. The reason for the cynicism is an inability to see that things can or will get better. Therefore, they begin voicing their hopelessness in cynical comments. They may say things like, *"Why are they asking our opinion; they're just going to do whatever they want,"* or *"We're never going to come back from this,"* or *"It's all office politics; nothing is going to change."* It is evident from these sorts of comments that your employees don't have any optimism, they don't believe their voice matters, and they don't see the possibility that things can get better. By camouflaging their comments in cynicism, they are voicing their defeat in a socially acceptable way, but this also can drag down the morale of other team members and cause a spirit of defeat to permeate the entire organization.

Often these individuals feel helpless, trapped or defeated. Their burnout has seeped into their spirit, and they've lost all motivation. This loss of motivation is another indicator of burnout. It's different from the temporary lack of motivation that you might notice in an individual after a particularly trying day or long week. Burnout-induced lack of motivation is much more pervasive; it infects all tasks and responsibilities equally and is not the result of fatigue or exhaustion that might be cured after a good night's rest. When an individual is burnt out, their lack of motivation may seems to be resistant to any attempted strategy.

Across the board, it will be met with insouciant non-responsiveness. Often this individual can't complete basic tasks, they can't pull it together to finish projects on-time, or raise funds for programs, they won't volunteer to take on new projects, and they might not even come to required meetings.

When an individual is burnt out, their lack of motivation may seem to be resistant to any attempted strategy

They are thoroughly disengaged, and it's the result of the stress they are experiencing on the job. Until that stress is managed or removed, it will be nearly impossible for them to find the motivation to do their work.

Another standout sign of burnout is decreased satisfaction accompanied by a low sense of accomplishment. We all like to feel that when we go to work, we are providing a valuable service, that the work we do has a net positive effect, and that we are moving toward some important and attainable goal. If your team members feel like they're spinning their wheels, but nothing is ever accomplished, they are at risk of burning out. This scenario is best illustrated in a story my mother once told me about her time in the Navy. At one point while she and her crew were docked, her officers ran out of things for them to do. As a solution, her superiors decided to have them paint the deck of the boat. That was a fine solution. They were proud of their unit, and that pride translated to the appearance of their boat, so they were happy to take on this task. However, as soon as they finished the first coat, they received the order to paint the boat again. When they finished the second coat, they were asked to do it again, not because there was anything wrong with the work, but because they simply needed to be kept busy. Their work no longer had any value aside from filling time. This endless painting was so frustrating for my mom that she asked to be transferred to a different unit.

I know you wouldn't put your team through this kind of tedious monotony, but it illustrates the power of doing meaningful work and accomplishing something you can be proud of. In my mom's case, once the deck was painted once, there was no longer any meaning behind the work. Her labor wasn't valued or even appreciated, so she simply had to leave for her own sanity, and possibly even to prevent burnout. As leaders, it is important that we are ever mindful of this difference. When we ask our team to do a thing, there is an understood agreement that it is because this thing is important in some way. If it turns out not to be, we've betrayed their trust. We've essentially told them without words that their work is not what's important, but only that they be working when they are on the clock no matter how unimportant that work is. This automatically establishes a mismatched sense of balance. We are saying, that when they've accomplished all of their tasks pressing at the moment, it is more important that they are engaged in a useless task (because it's a task) than for them to send a quick text to a child to ensure they got home from school okay and are starting their homework or that they take five minutes outside to recharge or take a moment to schedule a doctor's appointment. The default message has become, *"you must always be working whether or not it adds value because work is the most important thing."* Ironically, as it happens, an employee often performs better when they do have the autonomy to take a moment to re-center or to quickly handle a personal responsibility amidst their responsibilities. We actually strengthen our employees when we trust them to recognize what their priorities are and how best to accomplish them.

Behavioral Signs of Burnout

Aside from emotional responses, burnout will often manifest itself in how one responds behaviorally in the world. As the emotions that burnout brings settle into the body, soon behavioral changes start to show up. Sometimes, these behavioral changes are cries for help from the individuals on your team; other times they might not even be aware of why they are acting out until confronted. When you do notice these changes, it is a sign that you need to pay attention and start working to find solutions. The most dangerous and uncomfortable sign you will encounter is a staff member who has turned to food, drugs, or alcohol to cope with their stress. Often leaders will say, *"That's not in my wheelhouse; I'm not touching that subject."* On one level, there is some truth here. We are obviously not trained to deal with serious addiction problems or eating disorders, but we do have a responsibility to address and direct. By this I mean, that it is indeed your responsibility as a leader to confront the employee about the behavior and then point that person in the right direction so that he or she can get the help they need. It most certainly is our role to show our staff members that we care about them as people, not just as employees. We don't have to provide them with the answers, but we do want to make sure that we give them useful resources, are willing to find them the people who can best help, and that we are taking the time to document our conversation and follow-up with them. We don't want to wait until things are out of control and the team is suffering before we start to address the issue. By that point, it will likely be too late, and the employee may have already endangered their chance at continued employment and be suffering in their health.

We don't have to provide them with the answers, but we do want to make sure that we give them useful resources

I am by no means insinuating that the particular employee definitively stays with the organization. That is not actually something that falls within your responsibility to manage and will likely be sent up the chain. What I am saying, however, is that upon recognizing this behavior, it is your job to invest in the well being of the individual in whatever way you see fit, remembering also that this is likely a sensitive topic. Any conversations should be handled with care, sensitivity and respect for privacy, and should be addressed in tandem with your human resources department.

On a lighter note, another behavioral change that you might notice is an employee skipping work, coming in late, or leaving early. This is not something reserved only for face-to-face work. If this behavior is present, it will likely carry over to the virtual environment as well. This desire to simply not show up could be the manifestation of burnout. Similar to the way a lack of motivation presents, I'm not referring to a one-off case of being late or absent. Instead, it is a consistent pattern of absence. Perhaps this employee doesn't show up to team meetings or is always late for their shift. During a virtual meeting, it might mean leaving early, consistently turning off their video feed, actively disengaging from the content and discussion or consistently being distracted with another device. This distance is a clear sign of disengagement. What they're silently saying is, *"I'm here out of obligation only," "I'm not interested in contributing," "I'm not saying anything," "You can't see me,"* and *"I don't care enough to pay attention."* These are classic signs of disinterest. Often the stress that this person is experiencing has prompted him or her to decide to disengage before even logging on. A defiantly disengaged employee is burnt out, and is purposely stepping back. Often this tactic is their way of controlling one small aspect of a workload they feel they have no control over. If you find your employee has an issue with attendance or timeliness, it's time to assess burnout and find out where that behavior is coming from so that you can work on ways to fix the underlying problem.

Physical Signs of Burnout

Finally, we will explore some physical signs and symptoms of burnout. Burnout can and often does manifest itself physically. As we've learned more about mental health, we've come to understand that when our mental health is not in the best shape, there are physical signs that give us away. As we explore some of the signs and symptoms, let's remember that these physical signs are not exclusive to burnout and might mean there are other things that need to be explored with a medical professional.

One of the most telltale physical signs of burnout is intense lethargy. This is vastly different than being exhausted after having worked a sixty-hour week and feeling every one of those hours in your tired and aching muscles. This is a tiredness that stems from being pulled in so many directions, for so long that you are perpetually tired and drained.

With working from home becoming an emerging norm, it's safe to say that we've learned that the change of venue does not mean less stress; it only means less commute. Just because we can check off tasks from the comfort of our beds or while wearing sweatpants, does not take away the pressure. In fact, in some ways, it seems to have added additional pressure. Working from home comes with its own set of challenges, one of the biggest being, how to establish and maintain balance. When the computer is always within reach, it takes purposeful intention to shut it down and walk away. And it often opens the door to an expectation of being available round the clock. In this new environment, some employees are enticed to work more, mistakenly believing that just because an email comes in at 2am, that it must be answered at 2am. It is up to the leaders, to ensure that employees are encouraged to log off after they've put in their eight hours and to dedicate time to rest. For others, 2am might be the most convenient time to work, and that is fine as long it's clear it's not an expectation.

Another physical sign of burnout is a disrupted sleep pattern. If this becomes a consistent disruption, it can lead to decreased immunity and more frequent bouts of illness, as quality sleep helps to restore the body. Obviously, you cannot monitor how well an employee sleeps each night, but you can observe the signs of poor sleep. Perhaps they are relying on more coffee than normal or are physically looking sleep-deprived. If they are taking more sick days than normal, you might want to

Productive, effective and happy employees are also people who feel healthy and well

find out why the sudden change. Productive, effective and happy employees are also people who feel healthy and well generally speaking. If they are complaining of pain and fatigue, it could be that they are simply burnt out, and it is best that you address this to assess the need for change in workload or an allocation of needed resources.

The Four R's of Resilience

When burnout occurs, measures can be taken to "walk back" the burnout and alleviate the symptoms, but the most effective technique for combating burnout is to never cause it in the first place. The quality that does the most to combat burnout is resilience. As leaders, we create the ideal conditions for success by building a resilient culture. But first, we should break down what exactly it means to be resilient, and what characteristics we need to strengthen in order to develop it within our employees. In the sections below, I will go over what I've coined the *"The Four R's of Resilience."* When an individual feels these four sentiments are within their control, they will function better as a person and as a worker.

There is always the chance that when you hire someone, they come to you already possessing these qualities. And in that scenario, they will perform well for a period of time. But these qualities are not static. When an individual spends a substantial amount of time in an environment in which these qualities are not supported or appreciated, the qualities will soon begin to fade. It's important to know what the Four R's are and why they are important to maintain as the first step to achieving a resilient workforce.

Relevance

An individual who feels relevant knows what's important to them and allows their top values to guide how they live their life. Having a strong sense of what is relevant allows a person to know what serves them and what doesn't. They make decisions based on what is most important, not on a skewed sense of priorities.

An example of this is an employee who finds relevance in leaving work by 5:15pm because that ensures she will have a little alone time before everyone else arrives home. This alone time is important to her because it allows her to disengage and re-center before shifting her focus to the members of her family. She knows that when she doesn't get this time, she is more irritable, less present and not her best self. Because she values this time and knows the relevance of it, she would not return a client's call at 4:45pm both because she would not be able to give satisfactory attention to the client and because she'd also lose out on the crucial alone time that improves the quality of her relationships if the call ran long.

The qualities required to build the "relevance muscle" are self-awareness and strong values. You have to truly understand what's important to you in order to create a set of values that will govern your life and dictate how

What's relevant to you is not about work or career growth; it's the driving force behind those things that determines relevance

you're going to spend your time and energy. What's relevant to you is not about work or career growth; it's the driving force behind those things that determines relevance. Some common forces are family, friends, legacy, children, and life purpose. When we truly know what's important to us, we tend to be able to quickly decide if a situation warrants our time and attention or if it's merely a distraction. When we don't know what is relevant, we can easily find ourselves spending time on things that don't benefit us, and that don't contribute to our success or that feel out of alignment with our core values. When that happens, we are not working in authenticity. This is particularly important to you as a leader because you want your team members to have a strong sense of self and personal values. When those are in place and adversity arrives, they will use those senses to regulate their thoughts and emotions while relying on their values to overcome challenges.

Reason

As we move through life, there isn't always an obvious reason why something happens, especially something bad or disappointing. But generally speaking, the individual who can either find a reason or accept that a bigger reason, beyond their comprehension is present is far more resilient than the person who can't find or see a reason for the adversity they're facing.

When struggles arise, it's important to find the meaning that struggle has in our life. Though difficulties are unpleasant and sometimes traumatic, there is always a lesson to be learned or an experience worth sharing that can enlighten others. This could be a cautionary tale or a story of overcoming. Whatever the case, it's important to seek meaning and apply those lessons within our lives. Certainly, we don't want to go through adversity unnecessarily; however, if what we've gone through helps us help others, there is value to the struggle. This is true in our personal and professional lives. We've all shared a resource with someone so they could avoid making the same mistake we once made or so that they can better understand how to use that challenge to grow. When we use our experiences to guide others, it proves that our misstep actually had worth because we were able to pass on wisdom to someone else. No experience is a waste so long as we vow to look for the meaning within it and apply the lesson.

When I teach this concept in workshops, I'm often asked, *"How can you possibly find anything good about losing?"* This kind of question comes from how we view challenges. Unfortunately, in our society, you either win or you lose, and both are painted as opposing shades of good and bad. It's good to win and bad to lose. But in reality, it's not that black and white. Often, we learn a lesson that illuminates an area of personal or professional growth. It also can highlight a malfunction in our product or service. When we ask ourselves if a project went as planned, and the answer is, "no," it's not quite accurate to call the project a failure or to say that it was bad. When we look for reason and meaning, we can find the value in a failed project. And when we see things this way, we might recognize that the "failure" highlighted areas that need our attention but that have been perpetually overlooked. In our examination of it, we might even find the elements of what will become an even better solution. So it's in everyone's best interest to look at problems through the lens of "reason."

Response

Having an appropriate response to adversity is a hallmark of resilience. It can be very easy to react with unbridled emotion when something unexpected happens, but it can be much more difficult to respond rationally. Honing the ability to respond rationally to events leads to an improved ability to make wise and more thoughtful decisions. It also ensures that reactivity isn't driving all of our decisions, which can result in chaos and decreased morale.

Often when trials come our way, we see it as a materialization of the worst possible course of events playing out before us. But if we take a step back and look at the situation objectively, we often find that this is simply not true. It's actually just one set of possible events. The way out of any challenging situation is to objectively look at the facts in front you and remain positive. Additionally, being flexible ensures we are open to creatively find solutions to the problem. Optimism and open-mindedness are the pathways to resilience. If you can consistently remind yourself that things will get better, that you have everything you need in order to overcome the challenge, and that you're going to be better for having made it through this tough time, you'll find that problems don't take such a devastating toll on you. Additionally, getting information from reputable sources helps to keep your response to the situation grounded in reality. The last thing that you need in a crisis is to let your imagination invent possibilities and outcomes that are absent of fact and evidence. If we stay grounded, we can more effectively control our responses.

Responsibility

Resilient individuals understand first and foremost that they have a responsibility to themselves before anyone else. They understand that it is no one else's responsibility to make sure their personal needs are met. They don't see self care as selfish, and they make their wellbeing a priority. This quality will ensure an individual doesn't get swept up in following someone else's priorities, but that personal responsibility remains front and center.

Too often, we spend so much time caring for, helping, providing for, and giving to others, that we neglect our own needs. Our first responsibility is to ourselves. In order to be at our best, we need to take care

Our first responsibility is to ourselves. In order to be at our best, we need to take care of ourselves physically, emotionally, and spiritually

of ourselves physically, emotionally, and spiritually. Additionally, we must practice giving ourselves the time and attention we need to rest and recharge. We can't pour from an empty cup. Therefore, we have the responsibility to ensure we maintain good physical, mental and spiritual health. Each aspect of our health requires the same attention and care. It serves no purpose to be physically fit but mentally devastated. A person can't be efficient and productive if their mental or spiritual health is suffering. If you're not whole, you can't properly give of yourself to others. Additionally, it's important to advocate for those around you as well. We should be encouraging our colleagues and friends to adopt a life centered on self-care and resilient living practices.

Cultivating Organizational Resilience

In short, the most effective way to prevent employee burnout, thereby reducing the hefty cost associated with it is to build an environment where resilience is valued and prioritized. Leaders need to weave resilience into the very fabric of the company culture. If personal resilience is the individual's ability to rebound after adversity and cope with setbacks in a positive manner, then organizational resilience addresses how the organization itself weathers obstacles and adapts to change. Leaders must also ensure that they set policies, create environments, and model behaviors that reinforce a community where burnout is not the norm, but the exception.

This is how I define a resilient organization is one that has planned and prepared for adversity so meticulously that when setbacks and change come, the organization doesn't fold or break. Instead, it remains steadfast and confident in its policies, culture and most importantly in its team's ability to bounce back and thrive.

It is important for leaders to remember that resilience starts with the individual. If your team members don't practice personal resilience, it will be impossible for them to develop professional resilience. That means that as leaders, you need to promote the development of resilience in your current employees. We will get into the ways you can do that a little later.

It also means that going forward, you need to hire with resilience top of mind. Yes, I talked about resilience being a teachable and learnable skill, but that shouldn't mean that you hire first and teach resilience later. The more efficient method to cultivating a resilient culture is to build this into the hiring process. Don't be afraid to name resilience as a prerequisite in your job descriptions. When it comes time for the interview, ask pointed questions about resilience and assess where an individual is in real time. You will be able to tell a lot about their resilience from the way that they answer the questions. When you're confident that your new hire is indeed a resilient person, hire them but don't stop there. Make sure they recognize that they've joined a community that is equally as resilient and is dedicated to supporting them along the way.

Once you've created a team that is sufficiently resilient, both by hiring the right people and by training the staff you already have, you will be well on your way to creating a resilient organization. Resilient organizations don't happen my magic. They are formed from an abundance of resilient individuals, and they stay that way due to the diligence of the organization's leaders. As you probably guessed, resilience isn't a destination, it's achieved by making a consistent effort, practicing the *Four R's*, and making a daily choice to ensure these qualities are intertwined in the culture of your organization. Building resilience is an ongoing journey.

How to Inject Resilience into Your Organization

We've talked a lot about what resilience is and what qualities resilient individuals possess, but our goal is to actively create a resilient organization. We are now ready to look at how to effectively craft a resilient infrastructure within your company. We will go through the different areas where resilience needs to be evident and list specific ways in which you can ensure you are creating the right circumstances for resilient individuals to thrive. It may not be possible to implement all of these ideas overnight, but with a steady and dedicated effort, you have the power to make real change in your organization and reduce burnout considerably.

It might also be helpful to keep in mind that 13% of employee turnover is known to be due to burnout, but what is interesting is that there are many elements which contribute to burnout, some of which will go through below. It stands to reason that improving these additional factors of turnover like work environment, poor leadership, and no opportunity for growth, would improve employee turnover rates and decrease burnout.

☀️ Leadership

12% of Employee Turnover is due to Lack of Proper Leadership

Organizational resilience starts with leadership. No matter what other policies and structures you have in place, if your leadership doesn't value resilience and practice these ideas religiously, it simply won't permeate your culture. That is why it is critical that your leadership methods are effective and in line with your goals.

Teams need leaders to be flexible, transparent and appreciative.

Teams need leaders to be flexible, transparent and appreciative. These are not traits that they desire because they would be pleasant, though of course that's true. These are traits that employees seek out because when their leaders possess these qualities, it helps them perform their jobs better. For example, transparency is an essential leadership trait, during the pandemic this was especially necessary because employees wanted to know what was going on. At the time, we didn't have many answers for them, but the transparency of acknowledging this lack of answers didn't cause them to have less faith in us. Instead, when we told them we didn't have the answers, but were working on it as swiftly as possible, they respected our position and appreciated the honesty. In other words, transparency went farther than placating them with fabricated answers could have ever gone. Why? Because no one wants to feel like you are blowing smoke or end up highly disappointed when your promises turn out to be empty. It's important to be transparent to build your teams trust in you as a solid leader.

Cultivating appreciation is an area that many leaders struggle with. The challenge with appreciation arises because it is a very personal preference. Some employees like to be appreciated verbally, others with gifts cr rewards. Some people like to be appreciated in front of others at a meeting or event, while others prefer to be acknowledged quietly in a simple exchange or in a one-on-one meeting. Taking into account all of these different preferences, it can be difficult for management to get it right, and so the predominant reaction is to refrain from showing appreciation at all. However, this is not in line with creating a resilient culture.

Leaders need to practice appreciation consistently and in a variety of ways. Write notes, mention employees by name at meetings, affirm positive behavior with words in real time, have individual conversations, and occasionally hand out gift cards as acknowledgement. Once you start actually doing these things, if you're paying attention, you will see who responds to what. When you do assessments and listen to feedback, you will recognize what stands out for different employees. One person might recount a day when you told them what a great job they did. Others might rave about the time they got a handwritten card or a $5 gift card. As you get to know your team, you will learn what forms of appreciation work best with them, but even if you missed all the signs, you'd still have covered your bases through sheer variety and consistency. Once you start doing this, you'll notice a difference in morale right away. It's nice to be appreciated in all areas of life; work is no exception.

Leaders, themselves, should possess and utilize the *Four R's of Resilience*. Seeing this behavior modeled for them, employees will understand what is appropriate and expected. If they were to constantly see a superior overreact to problems or to blame bad situations on circumstances or other individuals, it would send the message that they should do the same. This would trickle down to everyone in the company and would eventually grow into feelings of negativity and malaise. Be the kind of employee that you'd like to oversee.

One common practice that should be avoided at all costs is micromanagement. Nothing is as damaging to a team as a leader who micromanages regularly. The primary message that this sends is that the leader or manager doesn't trust the team to do the work. Because there is no trust, leadership determines that they must insert themselves into the process to ensure everything goes as expected. Not only is this frustrating and exhausting, it is simply disrespectful, and it achieves the exact opposite goal of what's intended. Micromanagement tells our employees that we know better, that things can't get done right unless we are involved, and that our team is nothing more than our boots on the ground with no vision or agency of their own. Make sure your team knows they are trusted and respected to do what they were hired for.

Finally, let's talk about the simple, yet often overlooked *Golden Rule*; treat others as you wish you to be treated. Exhibiting resilience through leadership requires us to always be mindful of how we are treating our team, how we speak to them, how we care for them in times of need or crisis, and how we handle them when disciplinary action is needed. It's important to remember that resilient leaders practice being open to others' ideas and thoughts, maintain control over their emotions, and exhibit professionalism, even in difficult situations. The key is to keep kindness and respect at the forefront of your interactions with your team, colleagues and clients. Remember, your team is watching how you interact with everyone in the organization.

The key is to keep kindness and respect at the forefront of your interactions with your team, colleagues and clients

Questions to Ask Regarding Your Organization's Leadership

1. Are we being transparent with staff about issues that are important to them?

2. Are we flexible in unforeseen circumstances?

3. Does leadership make a consistent effort to show appreciation to team members when they do something commendable?

4. Does leadership practice what they preach?

5. Is leadership often micromanaging staff or do they generally trust staff to get the job done?

💡 Team

20% of Employee Turnover is due to
Lack of Career Development Opportunities

When it comes to your team, the most important message I can relay to you is that you need to hire for what's missing. The beauty of a team is that it is something that is created. In hiring, we compile of group of diverse individuals who all have different strengths, abilities and weaknesses. That all comes together in such a way where we literally have the power to create a group that is great at anything we desire, so long as we hire correctly. Too often, we hire to fill a position, and we haven't even taken the time to accurately list out what the requirements of that position really are. We know we need a role filled, and we dig out the template we used the last time we hired for that position or slightly edit the job description for the position we most recently hired for. We don't look at the overall makeup of the team, and pose the question: *What are we missing? What will make us a stronger team?*

And so the result is, we often get someone who is not quite a fit. But in the interest of reducing the time dealing with a vacancy, we settle for whatever individual shows up. I'd like to suggest another way to go about hiring, and there's one industry that excels in this area. That industry: sports. Take a look at any football or basketball team. They don't simply put out a job listing for a point guard or running back. They look at their team with an honest eye, and they ask themselves what they're missing. If a team is missing speed or a team leader or someone who can break tackles, those are the qualities they recruit for. This is why analysts are able to predict what decisions certain teams might make on draft day. If one team already has the best quarterback in the league, they are not going to recruit another quarterback, but if they've been alternating running backs all season and no one has quite stepped up, you can be sure they are looking to fill that very specific need.

The same philosophy needs to be true in your organization. Hire for what your team needs. If it comes down to two candidates who are equally qualified, but one has an ebullient demeanor and the other is more reserved, look at your team. Does your team need a cheerful and enthusiastic energy on the floor to boost morale or are they already pretty lively and could use someone who might reign them in a bit? That's how you make your final decision, not based on who you like more or who went to your alma mater. Your job is to create the best team possible. Who is going to be the best fit with you team? Who is going to provide the best value to the team?

Once you've got the right people hired, you've also got to make sure you've got the right people in the right positions, and that they have the right skillset for the job. The most surefire way to cause someone to burn out is to put that person in a position that is not suited to his or her strengths. If you have a person who is great at fundraising, but they are stuck in an administrative position, it won't be long before you see the repercussions of this mismatch. Not only will this individual become discouraged trying to handle responsibilities that he or she is not suited for, but your organization will miss out on utilizing the unique strengths that this person possesses. Sometimes people end up in positions that they are not a fit for because of earlier layoffs, or because they just wanted to get a foot in the door and misrepresented themselves. There can be any number of reasons for a mismatch. It is your job as a leader to identify the strengths of your existing staff and make sure they are utilized where they not only provide the biggest benefit to the organization, but also where they will naturally thrive and excel.

I once consulted with a nurse who got promoted to Nurse Director. Once in that position, she steadily began promoting members of her original team whenever an opening came about. Nurses that she formerly worked with were being promoted to supervisor. Now on the surface, there is nothing incredibly wrong with this, but when we take a closer look, we start to see the problem. She soon noticed that her turnover rate was increasing. No one was staying in the supervisor roles she was filling. That's when she came to me for help, and right away I could see the problem. She believed in promoting from within, and thought that she was doing a favor to all of her former colleagues by promoting them, but she had failed to ask a simple question. *Is a managerial role what these nurses want and excel at?* What was happening was that she was taking nurses who had always been patient-focused, and she was moving them into a role where they'd now be nurse-focused. A supervisor role is one in which the person must see value in creating a robust life for the nurses, which indirectly creates a better environment for the patients. So if a person doesn't see sending emails, sitting through meetings and performing other administrative tasks as a satisfying role and part of the bigger picture in caring for patients, then they simply wouldn't be effective at the job. And that was what was happening. I helped her understand that she would have better luck with retention if she hired individuals that saw their purpose in a leadership role that was one step removed from patient care. It's not about promotion for the sake of promotion; it's about filling the role with someone who is a passionate leader. It's important to understand that as a leader, your primary responsibility becomes talent management and sustainability. The client becomes secondary. Sure, everything we do goes back to providing a great experience for our clients, but as a leader, you are responsible for providing a great experience for your team, who in turn passes that greatness on to the clients.

It's important to understand that as a leader, your primary responsibility becomes talent management and sustainability.

It's also important when building teams to ensure that individuals have a strong character and are agile. Solid employees have the ability to pivot and change course without taking on a defiant or curt attitude. You also want to ensure that you're hiring team players who are decisive action takers. Your organization is better served when your team members actually want to work together, rather than when it's composed of individuals who are only interested in their own advancement. These same employees need to know how and when to take action so that leadership doesn't have to constantly step in and intervene.

One great way to support all of these traits is to participate in debriefing sessions. An institution I worked with implemented team debriefing, and quarterly they would take an anonymous patient case for us to debrief as a multidisciplinary team. We were presented with the case, and we had to work together to decide how it could have had a better outcome with no blame, just facts and open, honest discussion. As I spoke to colleagues in other organizations, I found this was not common, but in fact, most felt it would have been helpful to implement this strategy to learn and grow as a team.

Debriefing is a beneficial practice after both wins and losses. It helps everyone appreciate and celebrate the good things that occurred, and it also helps everyone reframe the areas that didn't go so well. You can get ahead of future problems, by looking at what went wrong and how it could've been prevented. Plus, partaking in sessions like these allows for everyone to be included and offer input, which is promotes resilience.

Questions to Ask Regarding Your Organization's Team

1. Do we have the right people in the right positions?

2. What is our hiring process like? Are we recruiting talent based on team needs and dynamics in addition to skillset?

3. What is our current employee turnover rate and what is it attributed to?

4. During interviews, are we asking specific questions about personal resilience?

5. Do we debrief as a team regularly?

💡 Policies & Procedures

12% of Employee Turnover is due to Poor Job Characteristics

The best way to find out how your policies and procedures are working is to ask your team. All policies and procedures should be created with the team in mind. After all, they are the ones who work most intimately with all of the procedures and who are often most affected by the policies. It only fits that they are involved in the process. By simply inviting their feedback and suggestions, you are creating an environment where they feel heard and valued. When it comes time to create new policies and procedures, don't delegate it to the bureaucrats or policymakers. Instead seek the advice and feedback of the actual people who will be asked to follow the new procedure or interact with the new policy. Then once it is implemented, have your team on the floor revise and provide feedback. Let them share input about what works and what doesn't, and then actually do something with that information. Sometimes policies or procedures are great ideas in theory, but when it comes to implementation, they fall short. Usually the first to recognize these shortcomings are your staff on the ground. They have practical knowledge rather than theoretical ideas, and their insights can drastically improve the policies and procedures you set in place. After all, if a policy has no efficacy, it is not adding value and could even be costing you time and resources.

In the creation process, you also want to make sure that you're creating procedures that are client-minded rather than client-focused. Sometimes when we focus solely on the experience for the client, we end up with a procedure that is unsustainable for the team. All procedures must be created with this balance in mind. Though the client may be happy with outcome of a certain policy, the team might find themselves frustrated and experiencing unnecessary stress. Simple changes could be made that still satisfy the majority of the clients, but simultaneously relieve frustrations of your team.

When it comes to policy-making, it's vital that policies line up with your organization's mission, vision and values. When this is out of balance, it shows. A common example in healthcare occurs in regard to sick notes. It's our job to write sick notes for patients we serve. We have no problem writing a note that recommends an individual take time off for any reason the provider deems valid, no matter how flimsy. But at our own organizations, many staff members are required to come into work sick. An employee can't simply take two days off for mental health because we will then require a note. This is a double standard. On one level, we claim that we espouse the idea of mental, physical and spiritual health, but when it comes to our department's schedules, we suddenly change our tune. This discrepancy doesn't go unnoticed, and the employees respond to it. They understand that though we say we care, when it comes down to real situations, we actually don't practice what we preach.

Let's look at another example: time-off requests. When an employee requests time off, most supervisors are not looking at that request through a lens of wanting to make it work. They look at the schedule, see the conflicts and make a decision based on the facts they are seeing in that moment. But envision the shoe on the other foot. How would it feel if you requested time off, and the person in charge looked, saw that it was not possible and denied your request without giving it a second thought? There has to be an element of fairness built into your system for accepting these requests. All employees should have the opportunity to take off for a holiday. Employees have earned time off to rest and recharge. Consistently denying this time or infringing upon an employee's time off does not promote resilience or prioritize self-care. Discrepancies like these need to shift if we hope to have more resilient employees.

Additionally, it's important to remain innovative. The procedures that we currently have in place don't need to last forever. If new technology comes along, and it can help with efficiency or thoroughness, don't hesitate to re-address old ways of doing things. The world is not stagnant, and the procedures that are in place need to reflect that reality. Add automation and innovation where you can. If you're in a non-profit industry, this can be hard to do while also taking into account tight budgets, but make it a point to do what you can when you can.

It's essential that when policies are created, that leadership make it a point to follow these policies as well. Nothing betrays trust more than creating an environment where what is good for one is not good for the other. It also sends the message that the policy is not important if the leaders themselves won't follow it.

Nothing betrays trust more than creating an environment where what is good for one is not good for the other

Any policies that are created should be wellness-driven. This means that the policies should strive to make the working conditions and results better, with attention placed on how these policies will affect the experience of its employees. Policies also need to be on brand. If a policy is created and completely goes against the core values of the organization or sends a different message than what is espoused in other literature, it needs to be revised or altered until it is on brand. The policies comprise a vital part of the organization, and if they send a message that is not what the organization stands for, they can do more damage than good.

Questions to Ask Regarding Your
Organization's Policies & Procedures

1. Is your team part of the process when it comes to developing or assessing policies and procedures?

2. Are your policies and procedures in line with your organization's mission, vision, values and central messaging?

3. Are you consistently incorporating innovation into your existing policies and procedures?

4. Does your entire leadership staff adhere to the policies and procedures set in place? Do your employees see this?

5. Is there a wellness focus to your policies? Do they take the employees wellbeing into account?

☀ Environment

6% of Employee Turnover is due to Poor Work Environment

When we talk about a resilient environment, we're primarily talking about mood building. The way in which an office area or workspace is set up contributes handily to the wellbeing and spirit of the workers. Things such as how the lights are distributed, what color paint is on the walls and what artwork is visible go a long way in creating the right mood amongst your staff.

The space itself should be wellness-focused. The clear message should be one of all-around wellness and health. This incorporates everything that is a part of the environment, from the lighting, to the desks, to the predominating smell. If for example, you allow people to smoke right in front of your doors, and the constant smell of cigarette smoke is infiltrating the workspace, it doesn't send the message that those working in that area are important and valued. Even something as simple as what snacks you offer in your vending machine play a role in the overall vibe of your organization. If all you are offering your team is old, high-calorie, sugar-laden vending machine snacks, you are not doing all you can to promote a sense of wellness. Are there healthier options, different machines, or other unique ideas that might send a different message?

One example I have about the importance of environment comes from my time working at a college call center. The office was an old automotive garage with no windows. The only source of light was artificial, the walls were dark, grey concrete, and the resulting overall vibe was soul-crushing. If we wanted a quick dose of natural sunlight, we had to go to the former auto bay and open the garage doors, but even than the light didn't reach the office so the joy was incredibly short-lived. We came up with some solutions such as repainting the walls and adding artwork of outdoor landscapes, and that helped a little. But the bottom line was that for a group that was the first contact many people had with the college, we were not treated to a particularly warm environment ourselves, and it took a toll on our job satisfaction.

When you are looking at and designing the space where your team will spend the bulk of their time, it's important to consider the effects of that environment on their spirit. Consider setups where employees can see each other, even if it's just through glass partitions, put thought into the paint color choices, and even consider what your bathrooms are like. Make food available to everyone that is free and accessible. Nothing is worse than working late on a project only to learn that you've missed lunch and there is no alternative. Having cans of soup or fruit options available is not only helpful for anyone in need of a bite, it says that you care that your team is fed and has what they need to be productive.

Do you have accessible coffee or tea options? In some hospital setups, the only good coffee is in the cafeteria, but the cafeteria is often an elevator ride and multiple hallways away. If the only coffee is fifteen minutes away, that is not an environment conducive to productivity, and it's not employee focused. There are simple solutions to these issues like installing high-end vending machines in key locations. Think of what you would like in a workspace and what little things would make your day better in even microscopic ways, then prioritize incorporating these touches. Trust me, it will go a long way.

Questions to Ask Regarding Your Organization's Environment

1. Is your employee workspace very closed off? Do the offices have doors that are often closed sending a message that others are not welcome?

2. What is the lighting like? Do you rely primarily on artificial lighting? Is there a way to incorporate more natural light?

3. Do you have free snacks, emergency meals and healthy vending machine options that are easily accessible?

4. What kind of chairs and desks are available to your employees? Do you have ergonomic options available? Are these easy to obtain or is it a tedious process to get a new chair or desk?

5. What is the overall vibe of your workspace? Is it a place that you would enjoy spending time in? If not, what can be done to improve it?

💡 Culture

12% of Employee Turnover is due to Poor Work/Life Balance

It's so important to foster a culture where people are respected and rewarded for the work that they do. One of the most common ways this practice is undone is by allowing bad apples to exist within your culture unchecked. When good employees see you tolerate an insubordinate employee, it sends a message not only that there is no accountability, but that the good work they've done has little value. This is a common scenario in some workplaces, and I find employers are afraid to reprimand an employee due to fear of litigation, bad press or other circumstances that could reflect poorly on the organization. While these are valid concerns that must accounted for, I would ask, *"What is it costing you, in terms of employee engagement, satisfaction, retention and burnout to allow this situation to occur?"* Because what's undisputed is that it is certainly costing you real dollars and cents. Tolerating and even protecting a bad employee will destroy the culture of your organization over time. As a leader, you must find an effective way to navigate this.

Every work culture should be equity driven. This means that everyone under your leadership should have everything that they need to do their job, and that the playing field is level. It also means inclusion; all employees should feel welcome to participate and contribute. The way that you can make sure this is happening is by ensuring equal opportunities and fair representation for everyone. Your team should represent not simply its clientele, but the population at large. Again, this goes back to identifying what your team is lacking and ensuring that you are actively trying to fill those gaps. Representation matters to your team and your clients.

Your team should represent not simply its clientele, but the population at large.

The culture should also be motivational, but this is a tricky area. Many leaders will tell you that motivating their team is one of the most challenging parts of their job. This is in part due to the uniqueness of our team members. A great leader has to find the motivating factor for each individual team member, and often that factor is different for everyone. Motivation therefore must be tailored. Obviously, that is going to require some time and energy on your part, but it will be worth it in the end. Some good ways to motivate your team could be including team-building activities, volunteering together on a service project or incorporating wellness programs into the workday. Because not everyone is the same, it is best to consult your team before making these decisions. Take some time to see what type of initiative excites them, where they'd like to volunteer their time or what wellness activity, they'd like to participate in.

The workplace culture also needs to promote the idea of self-care, serve as a connection hub and exhibit a sense of adaptability. In times of uncertainty, employees become highly conscious of how adaptable their organizations are in real time.

Employees will be taking inventory of how their needs are met, and if they are equipped with what they need to do their jobs remotely. When an organization can adapt in the face of challenges, employees feel secure and supported. This removes doubt and uncertainty, allowing the employees to focus on doing their job well in spite of adversity.

It's no secret that employees talk about their employers on social media. They speak loudly, and often candidly about their likes, dislikes and experiences. The things they say can have a profound impact on how an organization is perceived by potential new hires. Often with no other frame of reference, potential talent will use the reviews of past employees and customers to decide if your organization is a place they'd like to work. If you're losing out on qualified talent because you've fallen short of creating a culture of resilience and have allowed your reputation to falter, it is paramount that you work to remedy the problem. The financial ramifications of a poor organizational culture make it of the utmost importance stay in front of issues, and address them as they arise, before they make it to a consumer review or job search site.

As leaders, we have to do everything we can to shift our current culture to one of wellness and self-care. We need to ensure that our employees know without a doubt that we care about their wellbeing. We are in an era when the employers are no longer vetting the talent; it's the talent that is vetting the employer. With this being the case, we have to prove ourselves to the potential hires. This means doing and implementing things that stand out, things like building quiet rooms and implementing wellness programs. Employees need to feel like they are supported as a whole person when they choose to work for us, that we don't just care about what talents they bring to the organization, but that we care about who they are and what's important to them as a person.

Oftentimes, companies implement wellness programs, but they end up failing because they are underutilized. There are many possible reasons for the failure, but one possibility is that the program lacked incentive or was advertised poorly. A wellness program has to incorporate an incentive in order for people to invest in it, even if it benefits the employee physically to participate. It needs to be set up in a way where they get points for doing certain things, and those points eventually add up to a larger incentive such as a gift card or discount. Also, if you're offering programs after work, you may be missing an opportunity for maximum participation. Wellness programming should be offered during work hours or during lunch. This sends the message that you're willing to put profit aside in order to address your staff's health. That is a pretty powerful message. And the best part is that if you do invest that hour into your staff, you're nearly guaranteed to get that hour back, but you also get other benefits along with it. That's the kind of thing that employees tell their friends. The word gets out, and people start seeking your organization out as somewhere they want to work. That not only increases your pool of talent but adds to the overall efficacy of your team. Don't be afraid to think outside of the box. The payoff is long-term, and will stay consistent if you continue to put the effort in. Healthier teams mean reduced healthcare costs, increased satisfaction, decreased burnout, and overall cost savings.

Questions to Ask Regarding Your Organization's Culture

1. Is your organization inclusive? Are all employees treated fairly?

2. Is your team watching as you tolerate poor behavior and performance?

3. Are there programs and resources in place to help employees engage in self-care?

4. If you have wellness offerings, do you implement them during work hours or after? And is your wellness program incentivized?

5. Are you consistently connecting with employees to see what is and isn't working?

Strategies for Promoting Wellbeing

Once you understand the importance of creating a workplace that is structured in a way to promote resilience, you then must ensure that you're employing strategies that promote wellbeing on a daily basis. The only way to ward off burnout is to engage in these strategies consistently. I've listed some for you as a starting point.

Assess Burnout

The only way to promote wellbeing is to know when it is lacking, and the only way to do this is to assess burnout. You can do your best watching for the emotional, behavioral and physical signs that we went through earlier, but the most effective way to know for sure if an individual is suffering burnout is to simply ask. A Burnout Assessment tool is helpful in doing this. Oftentimes, being open to having the conversation and asking hard questions is enough of an acknowledgement to get the ball moving in the right direction. In your conversation, you can offer some ideas and strategies for them to implement in order to cope with the stressors of the job and reverse burnout. Don't be afraid to make burnout assessment a regular part of your Check-In program. A quick way to remember this is to use P.A.A.P. (Prevent, Assess, Address, Provide). It's a leader's role to help prevent burnout, assess team members for burnout, address burnout should it be identified, and provide resources to manage burnout.

Promote Life/Work Harmony

It's important to let your employee know that you care about them as a person. Be sure to make it clear that you understand that they are working to manage a personal life alongside of their work life, and that doing so successfully can be challenging. Be sure to use intentional language that highlights that their personal life and self-care needs take precedence over work. When they know that you recognize that, they can more easily rationalize giving their personal issues more attention at certain times. There will be times when life outweighs work, and other times when work outweighs life, but the thing that you can always work to maintain is a certain harmony between the two. Organizations that encourage this more realistic view of how we manage the many responsibilities we have, are promoting a culture of wellness and resilience. Freeing your employees of being locked into the juggling act we have traditionally tried to manage, allows them to feel confident in delegating responsibilities free of guilt. This can be a game changer for your team, normalizing delegation and reprioritization of home and work tasks as a measure of creating life/work harmony and success. It shows your team that you care about their stress level and that your goal is to provide resources to help them in this area.

Provide Mental Health Days

One way to reinforce a sense of support is to provide your employees with mental health days. This allows employees to take built in MHD without having to disclose a specific reason. The classification of sick days requires a reason, but a mental health day is just that – a day for mental health. Often employees feel they are obligated to provide a reason for time off, which prevents them from taking time off. Because they feel like they need a legitimate reason for regular time off, some opt not to take the time at all, while others feel forced to lie. Neither situation is ideal, and that choice is not something that you want to reinforce as leadership. By providing mental health days, you are sending the message that self-care is important enough to be a standard and an expectation. Sometimes, employees might not even use their mental health days; just knowing that they have them available can be enough to diffuse stress. This does not mean however that you shouldn't employ language consistently that reinforces the message that cashing in on these days is perfectly acceptable any time.

It's also perfectly within reason to gift time when you feel it's warranted. If you notice that a particular employee worked especially hard on a project or went the extra mile in some way, tell them to take a paid day off.

Promote a Culture of Wellness

Promoting a culture of wellness can look like a lot of different things, but the primary message is: individual first. In other words, whatever a person needs to feel good, be healthy and enjoy a high quality of life is prioritized. One example of this is leading with a disclaimer when you send an email outside of work hours. There might be a reason why you need to be handling this email at such an odd time, but you can make it clear that you don't expect a response until business hours, and that just because you are writing doesn't mean you expect they are paying attention to work emails at this time. This will take the pressure off and ensure that your employees know that you respect their time.

Of course, an even better way to get this message across is to simply not send emails at odd hours. Following the standards you expect is the most effective way to convey the importance of separating personal and work time. Of course, life happens, and this probably can't always be avoided, so the second-best solution is to make your expectations of your team crystal clear.

Offer Daily Mindfulness Activities

There are mindfulness activities available everywhere on the Internet. There are also practitioners who have partnered with organizations to provide mindfulness activities directly to staff. If you choose to go this route, it can be as simple as sending a mindfulness activity via email or text to your staff daily. Encourage your staff to engage with the emails and activities and to constantly monitor their level of mindfulness. These activities are a simple way for you to both display your commitment to your team's wellbeing, and to offer methods of self-care. Not every mindfulness activity will resonate with everyone, but invariably some will resonate with some people, and that is perfect. It can be one of these small activities that prevent an employee from descending into burnout, and if that's the case, it is absolutely worth it.

Provide Resources

Ensure that you provide your team with a list of resources they can access for different issues. This might seem like a small thing, but by taking this proactive step, you are showing your team that you've listened to staff in the past, and compiled resources in order to anticipate their needs. This can be community resources for food, clothing or financial assistance or personal and professional development course opportunities. It can also be preparing a list of restaurants that deliver lunch in the area, best coffee or well-lit parking garages for those working late hours. Having these resources available highlights your willingness to help your employees during tough times and as they get oriented to their new workplace.

Revise or Create an EAP Program

If you have an existing Employee Assistance Program, consider making it more robust. If you don't have one, plan to create one. Talk with HR, and find out what they can offer your team. Once you have this in hand, determine what your team will actually use, ask them what they think they need and find out what isn't useful. Then make sure that it's accessible to everyone. An EAP is not good if no one uses it or if it's full of things that no one needs or wants. Work to make your EAP as good as comprehensive and useful as possible.

Limit Zoom Meetings

Zoom meetings might seem like innocuous gatherings that don't cause much damage to staff morale, but in this new normal, Zoom meetings are becoming a liability. Because they are so easy to access, they are becoming almost too prevalent. We assume that it's so easy to join, that we might as well invite everyone, and have as many meetings as possible to keep everyone informed and engaged. But the truth is that employees are being overwhelmed by the abundance of Zoom meetings. What we see as a simple check in and connection meeting is actually the final straw for a person who is trying their best to manage many other responsibilities.

As leadership, you are in the position to assess Zoom meetings. Whenever you are planning on a meeting (and this can apply to in-person meetings as well), ask yourself three questions.

- Do we need to meet to discuss this?

- Can any of this be done by email?

- Is it essential that everyone on the invite list be invited?

Once you begin asking these questions, you might find that you require far less Zoom meetings or that the list of invited team members shrinks. Just because these meetings are easy does not mean they are necessary. Maintain the sanity of your team and yourself by meeting only when it truly makes a difference.

Conclusion

As you might've noticed, there is a common thread that underlies the entire concept of building organizational resilience. That is — treating the members on your team as complex individuals deserving of your respect and support. If you take nothing else away from this book, please take that.

People have an abundance of options when it comes to where they can and want to work. It's not the same template that our predecessors faced when the mentality could afford to be "anything goes" as long as the needs of the business are met. Now we understand as employees and as leaders that people perform their best when they feel supported and valued.

People feel good when they know their work has meaning, and when they see how that work helps others. When people feel good, the room lights up, creativity can flow, and ideas seem to pour out like a waterfall. People need to feel positive energy to optimize their own positivity.

We know that burnout is a real problem, and we can see how costly it is. But it's not just costing money — burnout costs happiness, everyone's happiness, and not just the individuals actually burning out. I'll give you another sports analogy. We've all seen games where a miscommunication on defense turns into a turnover and a basket for the opposing team and so it goes until the game is nearly unbearable to watch. This chain reaction of poor performance is not reserved for sports. It's a real phenomenon. That's how burnout affects your team — it's contagious. It begins to feel like nothing is working, and it's tough to sit on the bench and support your team after every subsequent failure. These ruts are difficult to correct in the span of one game. Sometimes an especially motivating half time speech can change the course of things, but more likely, something dramatic needs to shift from within. But then you have those games and teams where everyone is on their "A" game, feeling good about their role in the bigger picture – it's those games where everything seems to flow like magic.

It's no different in the workplace. That is what your goal is as a leader. You're looking to find that magic. It's amazing that it has taken us this long to start recognizing the importance of a strong, resilient work culture. Now that you know, don't you want to do all you can to support it? None of it is actually difficult. It's just about doing things differently and being accountable. Let's build resilience into your organization and improve not just your bottom line, but the work and personal lives of your entire organizational team. Are you with me?

To unpack this on a deeper level, I offer one-on-one coaching and organizational consulting to support you in developing and implementing Resilience Based Leadership.

I look forward to hearing from you. You can reach me at:

Email: Rasheda@RashedahatchettMedia.com

Or visit me for Consulting at:

www.RashedaHatchettMedia.com/Consulting

Appendix: References

[1] Shane McFeely and Ben Wigert, "This Fixable Problem Costs U.S. Businesses $1 Trillion," 2019, https://www.gallup.com/workplace/247391/fixable-problem-costs-businesses-trillion.aspx#:~:text=A%20trillion%20dollars.,year%20due%20to%20voluntary%20turnover.&text=So%2C%20a%20100%2Dperson%20organization,to%20%242.6%20million%20per%20year.

[2] OC Tanner Learning Group, "Performance: Accelerated," n.d., https://www.octanner.com/content/dam/oc-tanner/documents/global-research/White_Paper_Performance_Accelerated.pdf

[3] American Psychological Association,. (2020). https://dictionary.apa.org/burnout

[4] Deloitte,. (2018). Workplace Burnout Survey. https://www2.deloitte.com/us/en/pages/about-deloitte/articles/burnout-survey.html

[5] Karlyn Borysenko. *"Burnout is Now An Officially Diagnosable Condition: Here's What You Need to Know About It."* Forbes. May 29, 2019. 9

[6] Eric Garton. *"Employee Burnout is a Problem with the Company, Not the Person."* Harvard Business Review. April 6, 2017. https://hbr.org/2017/04/employee-burnout-is-a-problem-with-the-company-not-the-person

[7] Karlyn Borysenko. *"How Much Are Your Disengaged employees Costing You?"* Fobres. May 2, 2019. https://www.forbes.com/sites/karlynborysenko/2019/05/02/how-much-are-your-disengaged-employees-costing-you/#30c330503437

[8] T. F. Mahan, D.A. Nelms, Y.Jeeun, A.Jackson, M.Hein, and R.Moffett, "2020 Retention Report: Trends, Reasons & Wake Up Call" (Franklin, TN: Work Institute, 2020), https://workinstitute.com/retention-report/.

www.ingramcontent.com/pod-product-compliance
Lightning Source LLC
Chambersburg PA
CBHW071140280326
41935CB00010B/1302